ECONOMIC ISSUES 7

Sterilizing Capital Inflows

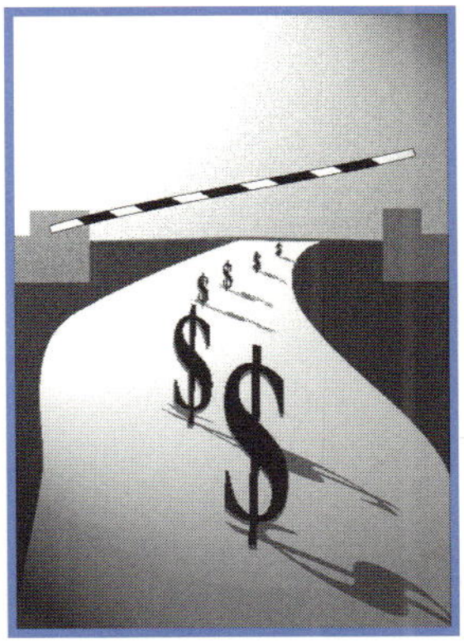

Jang-Yung Lee

INTERNATIONAL MONETARY FUND
WASHINGTON, D.C.

ISBN: 1-55775-632-5
Published February 1997

To order IMF publications, please contact:
International Monetary Fund, Publication Services
700 19th Street, N.W., Washington, D.C. 20431, U.S.A.
Tel.: (202) 623-7430 Telefax: (202) 623-7201
Internet: publications@imf.org

Preface

The Economic Issues series was inaugurated in September 1996. Its aim is to make available to a broad readership of nonspecialists some of the economic research being produced in the International Monetary Fund on topical issues. The raw material of the series is drawn mainly from IMF Working Papers, technical papers produced by Fund staff members and visiting scholars, as well as from policy-related research papers. This material is refined for the general readership by editing and partial redrafting.

The following paper draws on material originally contained in IMF Working Paper 96/53, "Implications of a Surge in Capital Inflows: Available Tools and Consequences for the Conduct of Monetary Policy," by Jang-Yung Lee, an economist in the IMF's Monetary and Exchange Affairs Department. Neil Wilson prepared the present version. Readers interested in the original Working Paper may purchase a copy from IMF Publication Services ($7.00).

Sterilizing Capital Inflows

Many developing countries have reaped handsome rewards from surging capital inflows in recent years. This is widely regarded as a very welcome phenomenon, raising levels of investment and encouraging economic growth. But surging capital inflows can also be something of a double-edged sword, inflicting rather less welcome and destabilizing side effects, including a tendency for the local currency to gain in value, undermining the competitiveness of export industries, and potentially giving rise to inflation. Why inflation? Capital inflows result in a buildup of foreign exchange reserves. As these reserves are used to buy domestic currency, the domestic monetary base expands without a corresponding increase in production: too much money begins to chase too few goods and services.

To ease the threat of currency appreciation or inflation, central banks often attempt what is known as the "sterilization" of capital flows. In a successful sterilization operation, the domestic component of the monetary base (bank reserves plus currency) is reduced to offset the reserve inflow, at least temporarily. In theory, this can be achieved in several ways, such as by encouraging private investment overseas, or allowing foreigners to borrow from the local market. The classical form of sterilization, however, has been through the use of open market operations, that is, selling Treasury bills and other instruments to reduce the domestic component of the monetary base. The problem is that, in practice, such sterilization can be difficult to execute and sometimes even self-defeating, as an apparently successful operation may raise domestic interest rates and stimulate even greater capital inflows. Unfortunately, many developing countries also lack the tools available to run a classical sterilization policy, or find it simply too costly to do so. This is often the case wherever the financial system is not fully liberalized.

Some countries have therefore turned to less conventional, supplementary measures. These measures vary from wider-band exchange rate policies and forward exchange market intervention to capital controls, such as variable deposit requirements and interest equalization taxes on foreign borrowings. Often, countries have turned to a so-called "belts and braces" strategy, which combines the indirect instruments of monetary policy with some capital controls.

This paper examines the experience with large-scale and sustained capital inflows in Chile, Colombia, Indonesia, Korea, Spain, and Thailand at various times in the past ten years. It looks at the practical limits to sterilization policy and then discusses various supplementary techniques, including foreign exchange swaps. In general, it finds that although classical sterilization operations can be effective for a time, the use of supplementary measures, including some indirect capital controls, may also be both desirable and effective. It also finds that these measures are usually most effective when imposed in the less distorting form of a tax rather than in outright restrictions on the quantity of capital flows. Moreover, tax revenues raised can be helpful in offsetting some of the costs.

Large-Scale Capital Inflows

Various factors underlay the surge in capital inflows in the six countries under review. In most of them, and notably in Korea and

Spain, the surge coincided mostly with faster financial liberalization, particularly a shift to allowing foreigners to acquire domestic stocks and bonds. In some cases, such as Thailand, where the capital account was already open, lower taxes stimulated a surge of investments by nonresidents. In Chile, Colombia, and Thailand, higher interest rates led to a wide differential in favor of the domestic market, also stimulating a surge of capital inflows. In several cases, expectations of exchange rate appreciation, or even of a stable exchange rate pattern, also reduced the discount at which the domestic currency was trading in the forward foreign exchange market, tempting foreign investors to "lock in" attractive interest rate differentials.

In response, all six countries initially resorted to some form of sterilized intervention, primarily through open market-type operations in the local bond markets. In Colombia and Korea, open market sales were accompanied by increases in reserve requirements or by tightened access to the central bank refinancing facility. These measures had limited effect. In many cases, the policy could not be applied indefinitely because the stock of open market bills rose too sharply, swamping the domestic market's ability to absorb them. In thin and illiquid local markets, central banks also found that open market operations could often be not only costly but also ineffective (resulting in higher interest rates that attracted yet more capital inflows).

As a result, most of the countries gradually stopped using open market sales as part of their sterilization efforts. They began, instead, to modify underlying policies. Thailand tried fiscal adjustment. Chile, Colombia, and Spain eased restrictions on capital outflows. Colombia and Korea accelerated trade liberalization. Chile and Spain introduced more flexible exchange rate policies, allowing for some nominal exchange rate appreciation. Indonesia attempted a more novel sterilization technique, using foreign exchange swaps, and Thailand tried adjusting government deposits (switching them from the banking system to the central bank). Many of the countries also tried to combine traditional monetary policies with some indirect capital controls. Variable reserve requirements on certain categories of foreign borrowing (imposed in Chile, Colombia, and Spain) have been the commonest form of such controls.

Practical Limits to Open Market Operations

There are several key limitations on the use of open market sales for sterilization purposes. Most notable, perhaps, is that the ability to sterilize has an inverse relationship with the degree of international capital mobility. If capital is highly mobile, attempts at sterilization may prove futile, because they can be rapidly overwhelmed by renewed inflows. While such a policy may be useful temporarily, it cannot work for long if the capital inflows persist, because sterilization can deal only with the effect rather than the underlying cause of shocks to the system. Also, the scope for classical open market operations may be severely restricted by the instruments available, particularly in developing countries, which are unlikely to have well-developed financial markets. In particular, Treasury bills or central bank paper may be an imperfect substitute for the financial assets foreign investors actually want to hold, such as stocks or bonds. Even if sterilization pushes up interest rates, which may in itself encourage more inflows, the prices of these preferred assets, which are in limited supply, may still continue to rise, accelerating the inward flow. In practice, policy is often limited by an inadequate supply of marketable instruments, or by thin and segmented local market conditions.

Finally, and not to be overlooked, is the heavy fiscal cost that may eventually derail the sterilization effort. Issuing a large stock of securities in an attempt to mop up the inflowing liquidity often places a heavy debt-service burden on the government or central bank. In some cases, such as in Chile and Colombia, it has led to a deterioration in the fiscal or quasi-fiscal balance (which includes the accounts of parastatal enterprises). For a central bank, operating losses can occur when the funds it raises are invested in foreign assets, which earn prevailing interest rates in the major world currencies—often lower than rates the central bank must pay on the bills it has sold. Large-scale losses can even lead to the need for a recapitalization of the central bank. In a worst-case scenario, the building up of a central bank or Treasury balance sheet may also expose it to greater credit risks, making the whole system more vulnerable to a sudden reversal in capital flows. This is more likely where much of the capital inflow is in the form of short-term portfolio investment, which can be reversed much more quickly and easily than foreign direct investment.

Supplementary Sterilization Measures

Without the instruments needed to execute open market operations, or when opportunities to use open market sales have been exhausted, central banks are forced to turn to other measures to control the money supply. Such supplementary tools include tightening the access of banks at the discount window, adjusting reserve requirements or the placement of government deposits, and using a foreign exchange swap facility. In theory, each of these expedients holds out the prospect of achieving the same effect as open market operations. In practice, each has both advantages and disadvantages.

Discount Policy and Directed Lending

One supplementary means to contract the money supply is to increase the cost or restrict the access to central bank credit. However, discount policy cannot be expected to play a prominent role as a flexible policy instrument. In many developing economies, rediscounts and loans granted by the central bank are often an automatic tool for priority lending extended via commercial or specialized banks to specified sectors of the economy. When this is the case, the rediscount ratio can still be adjusted, but not very often, because the results will be counterproductive to the goal of providing cheap credit to targeted sectors. Unless these subsidies are fully eliminated, rediscount facilities thus cannot be relied upon as a flexible tool. Even if credit available through the discount window is not subsidized, the central bank may still be loath to make aggressive changes in rediscount rates. This is often because the elasticity of demand for credit is very low, which means the demand for credit will not necessarily fall in response to higher rates.

Changes in discount rates do have some advantages over open market operations. They often cause a smaller fiscal cost, for instance, because discount rates are normally lower than market rates. They should also have a smaller impact on market rates, because the use of rediscount facilities, unlike open market operations, has no direct impact on local money markets. This is one case where a weak link between official discount rates and bank lending rates—which is often the case in developing countries—works to the advantage of the central bank. If the link is weak, then the sterilization objective may be achieved without raising local market interest rates by much, curtailing the incentive for further capital inflows. How much changes in discount policy can be used, however, may also be limited by likely effects on the central bank balance sheet.

Reserve Requirements

Increasing statutory reserve requirements—the proportion of assets that commercial banks must hold on deposit with the central bank—is another method of limiting the expansion of credit. In some countries, such as Colombia (1991), reserve requirements have been raised sharply to try and sterilize capital inflows.

Reserve requirements are either a remunerated requirement, when the central bank pays interest on the deposits, or an unremunerated requirement, when commercial banks receive no return. The effect of increasing requirements to sterilize capital flows is substantially the same as with open market operations. When interest is paid at or close to market-determined rates, the cost is likely to be much the same as with open market sales of interest-bearing instruments.

Reserve requirements have several practical limitations. Some banks may already hold reserve assets in excess of statutory requirements. Alternatively, the presence of weak "problem" banks, numerous in developing countries, may make higher requirements difficult or dangerous to implement. Colombia and Korea have found that raising the requirements is sometimes not feasible because they are already at a high level—owing to previous attempts to sterilize inflows. Reserve requirements are also quite a blunt tool for short-term liquidity management, because frequent changes can be highly disruptive to the efficient management of bank portfolios. Finally, in economies that are trying to liberalize their financial markets, to change reserve ratios is often seen as sending the wrong signal. They are in effect a tax on banks, and may cause financial disintermediation—with financial activity moving outside the banking system—weakening the central bank's monetary control.

Government Deposits

Another way to absorb reserves is to shift public sector deposits from commercial banks to the central bank. Where public sector deposits account for a large slice of the banking system's deposit base, as in Malaysia and Thailand, the use of this method has been highly effective in sterilizing capital inflows. An additional attraction is that, unless the interest paid on government deposits is higher at the central bank than at the commercial banks, there is no fiscal or quasi-fiscal cost.

Making transfers of government deposits is not without a downside, however. If the transfers to and from are frequent and unpredictable, uncertainty is much greater for commercial banks. As with frequent changes in reserve ratios, this makes it harder for them to manage portfolios efficiently. The use of this technique is also limited by the availability of government deposits. In some countries, government deposits must always be held at the central bank by law. In others, some types of public sector deposits are not within the government's control.

Foreign Exchange Swaps

Trading in the foreign exchange market can be used by a central bank in a way similar to open market operations in the domestic market. One method for sterilizing capital inflows is to do a foreign exchange swap in which the central bank agrees to sell foreign exchange against the domestic currency and simultaneously agrees to buy it back at a specified date in the future, using the forward exchange rate. Banks that buy the foreign currency may lend it to domestic residents or invest it abroad, but the effect is the same: it reduces the domestic currency base. The swap facility may be specifically designed to give an incentive to banks to "export" the funds, generating an offsetting capital outflow. This can be achieved by pricing the swap in such a way that the difference between the spot rate and the forward rate is bigger than the interest rate differential between the foreign and domestic markets.

Foreign exchange swaps have the advantage of being highly flexible. If the swaps market is liquid, they can be traded whenever necessary at prevailing market rates in a similar way to open market operations in the domestic market. Swap contracts can also be varied in length to reflect expectations about the duration of capital inflows and the need to offset them. Normally, foreign exchange swaps have a short-term maturity, but can usually be "rolled over," enabling the central bank to adjust flexibly to changing conditions. Unlike with open market operations, they can be executed without the need for a large stock of short-term government securities at the central bank, which is often the case in countries not running budget deficits. To prevent foreign capital from flowing back in at maturity, the central bank can also encourage the principal and interest from portfolio investments overseas to be reinvested in foreign markets.

Despite all these apparent advantages, such swaps are still little used, indicating that they also have disadvantages. The most obvious is that, like open market operations, they can cause losses for the central bank, especially when it is giving away favorable margins on the interest rate differentials. There is also a risk that foreign exchange sold by the central bank could be covertly sold back against the local currency, nullifying the intended effect. This type of "opposite transaction" can become a popular game for commercial banks, especially when they are being offered favorable margins. It can, however, be addressed by strengthening monitoring and supervision to ensure compliance; or by imposing restrictions on how banks can trade the swap proceeds.

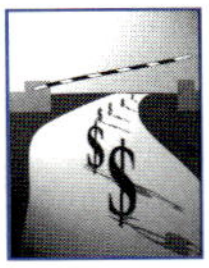

Other Measures, Including Indirect Capital Controls

After exhausting the above menu of supplementary tools, many developing countries have turned to various other techniques to try and sterilize capital inflows. These range from the introduction of a "wider band" exchange rate policy to intervention in the forward exchange market and, in more extreme circumstances, indirect capital controls, such as variable deposit requirements and interest equalization taxes. In many cases, the authorities who introduced the latter measures have believed that the side effects of sterilization policy could be reduced, and that the results would be less distortionary and more transparent, if they were not in the form of direct restrictions on the quantity of capital flows.

Wider Exchange Rate Bands

In response to large and persistent capital inflows, Chile (1992) and Colombia (1993) have widened the exchange rate band for their currencies. The most obvious benefit of doing this is that, by allowing some exchange rate appreciation, import prices tend to fall. With import prices dropping, there is downward pressure on inflation, so reducing the need to sterilize all capital inflows. A wider band may also reduce inflows that are stimulated by perceptions that the currency is undervalued—and expose such speculators to greater risk of short-term fluctuations. If the appreciation is rapid, this should also reduce the incentives for domestic speculators. Above all, a wider band allows the central bank more flexibility for intervention in the foreign exchange market, which can be important if there is a sudden reversal of sentiment.

On the debit side, a wider band can be disruptive to the economy as a whole. If a wider band allows changes in the exchange rate that are well anticipated, then of itself it can provoke large and sudden inflows or outflows of capital. It can also have the perverse effect of stimulating expectations that the rate may devalue, if the market believes that the central bank is trying to improve export competitiveness rather than to bear down on inflation. In short, it can be difficult to send out clear and reliable policy signals, especially if the previous policy was anchored on the basis of a stable exchange rate.

Intervention in Forward Exchange Market

Foreign exchange swaps, as discussed earlier, are not the only way for a central bank to intervene in the foreign exchange market. An older and more commonly used technique is to make "outright" forward exchange transactions via a forward exchange facility.

By offering a forward exchange facility, the central bank gives domestic investors the opportunity to "hedge" the value of their foreign investments by locking in a forward exchange rate. It can thereby encourage offsetting capital outflows. However, this sounds a lot easier in theory than it often is in practice. For one thing, the central bank needs to develop a liquid and well-functioning forward market in foreign exchange. As with other financial instruments, many developing countries lack such well-developed forward markets.

Offering a forward exchange facility can also be risky. To the extent that it exposes the central bank to financial losses, it can have fiscal costs. To avoid such costs, the central bank needs to refrain from offering excessively favorable premiums above the existing interest differentials.

In the long run, the best way to make forward exchange intervention more effective is to encourage the private sector's demand for forward transactions, enhancing the liquidity and efficiency of the forward market. One method for doing this (as adopted in Korea in 1994) is to relax the documentation criteria (known as the "real demand" principle) for eligibility to make forward transactions. The ceilings on forward transactions can also be raised progressively, in line with an increasing volume of international transactions.

Easing Restrictions on Capital Outflows

A number of developing countries have tried various ways to offset capital inflows by relaxing controls on capital outflows. Relaxing restrictions on outflows may include such measures as easing surrender requirements on foreign exchange earnings, permitting local institutions to make investments abroad, or allowing nondomestic entities to issue local-currency bonds in the domestic market. Such measures will only work, of course, if the restrictions were effective in the first place. If so, then they do offer a number of potential advantages. They can, for instance, increase the overall efficiency of investments made by local institutions, allowing for some international diversification of their portfolios. Exporters can also benefit by being allowed to retain foreign currency earnings abroad, helping them to manage their foreign assets more efficiently. The issuing of bonds by international organizations (such as the International Finance Corporation) may have ancillary advantages too, such as promoting further development of the local financial market. Above all, simplifying the process for remitting profits and income may send a positive signal about the ability to move capital in and out, which may lower the risk premium on all the country's financial assets.

Unfortunately, such measures may also be self-defeating. Simplifying the process for exporting capital, for instance, may of itself increase confidence in the exchange system, encouraging more inflows. Alternatively, in countries that have accumulated large external debts, such changes could exacerbate the threat of a large and prolonged current account deficit.

Variable Deposit Requirements

To discourage capital inflows, recourse has been made by a number of countries to the introduction of a deposit requirement, whereby a certain percentage of foreign currency borrowed by domestic residents must be placed with the central bank in interest-free, non-assignable deposits for a fixed period. This effectively serves as a tax on foreign borrowing. It is akin to a nonremunerated reserve requirement, but denominated and paid in foreign currency. Generally regarded as a form of capital control, it can also be viewed as a sterilization instrument because it directly sterilizes a fraction of capital inflows and, as such, can offset some of the cost of other sterilization measures. Unlike open market operations, it does not have any direct impact on domestic interest rates and so does not directly risk perpetuating the capital inflows. It can also be regarded as market-based, since it is not so extreme as a direct prohibition, like an embargo. Because it affects only the yields or costs of capital inflows, it is generally regarded as superior to direct controls or restrictions on the quantity of capital allowed to flow in.

The percentage and the deposit holding period can be varied, and may be adjusted frequently in response to changing conditions. One major advantage is a built-in feature that penalizes short-term borrowings more severely. Such short-term borrowings are normally considered to be the most destabilizing form of capital inflows. The requirement can also be modified, such as by placing a higher ratio on short-term borrowings, so that its disincentive effect is targeted even more precisely at "hot money" inflows that are seeking short-term gains. The nonremunerated feature of such deposits can help offset the central bank's operating costs on other sterilization operations. And, by locking up a portion of the capital flowing in, this also reduces the need for other costly sterilization measures.

Despite these considerable advantages, a variable deposit requirement also carries all the disadvantages that go with capital controls. The most obvious is that borrowers will probably seek to circumvent it by seeking out loopholes. It can also misallocate resources. Borrowers may be unable to take advantage of lower interest rates in international markets, for example, because of the extra costs imposed by the deposit requirement. It may also exert an uneven impact on the availability of low-cost funds, penalizing firms that engage in international trade over firms involved only in the domestic market. Some critics also complain that a variable deposit scheme hurts not only "speculative" but also "genuine" investments, because it increases uncertainty for all borrowings in foreign currency.

Whether variable deposit requirements are effective and, if so, whether they work for long are both controversial issues. However, empirical evidence from the six countries studied would suggest that they are at least partially effective. In particular, the evidence would suggest that countries that lack well-developed open market instruments are at least able to buy time by using variable deposit requirements—until they are able to work out whether the inflows are transitory.

Interest Equalization Taxes

Unlike variable deposit requirements, interest equalization taxes can have a direct impact on both inflows and outflows of capital. When imposed on outward-bound transactions, the tax is imposed on the acquisition of foreign securities by domestic investors. Traditionally, the interest equalization tax has been used in precisely this way in order to level the yields between domestic and foreign securities, so discouraging local investors from buying foreign assets. If applied for capital inflow purposes, it could be called a "capital import tax." For foreign investors, the tax effectively lowers the rate of return they get on local assets. And for domestic companies or others who are borrowing overseas, it effectively increases the cost of foreign capital, bringing it more into line with local rates.

For the policymaker, the main advantage of the tax is that it can exert an influence on the exchange rate without the need for changes in interest rates or intervention in the currency markets. There are, however, many wider economic issues that are raised by the precise design or operation of such a tax, including whether short-term transactions should be taxed more heavily than long-term transfers and whether public debt should be exempt.

The United States and Brazil are among the few countries that have imposed interest equalization taxes on trading in financial assets between residents and foreigners. Thailand adopted a slightly different approach, intermittently applying a 10 percent withholding tax on interest payments to foreigners. Another variant was the "thin capitalization provision" adopted by Australia in 1987. This penalized offshore borrowings by prohibiting the tax deductibility of interest payments on foreign loans whenever such loans exceeded a stipulated proportion of a firm's total capital.

In the United States, the tax was seen as an instrument to stem an outflow of U.S. dollars stimulated by higher returns on foreign stocks and bonds. After first being applied as a temporary measure in 1964, it was repeatedly extended until finally being dropped ten years later. The authorities kept extending the tax partly in the belief that it was effective in reducing investment overseas, especially during a period of continued balance-of-payments deficits. However, it did require continual amendments as investors found more and more ways to get around it.

In Brazil, a tax introduced in 1993 primarily because of concerns about capital inflows was intended mainly to discourage heavy borrowing abroad by Brazilian companies through the placement of bonds on international markets. In November 1993, the newly created Foreign Capital Fixed Income Fund became subject to a financial transaction tax of 5 percent, payable at the time capital enters the country. The proceeds of foreign borrowings through the placement of notes, bonds, and commercial paper—when converted into local currency—was also made subject to a transaction tax of 3 percent. In December 1993, a uniform withholding tax of 15 percent was also imposed on profits, dividends, and bonuses for all foreign capital. The effect was immediately visible, with new bond issues falling sharply in the first quarter of 1994.

An interest equalization tax may thus be an effective way to deal with destabilizing capital flows. The U.S. experience, however, suggests that such a tax should probably be used only as a temporary measure, because its effectiveness tends to erode as investors find ways to circumvent it. This is perhaps reflected by the experience in Brazil since 1994, where the precise tax levels have been adjusted several times—at various times increased, reduced, suspended, and then reimposed.

The interest equalization tax also shares the disadvantages of other capital controls, including the administrative costs of implementation, the fact that it can raise the cost of capital generally, and its tendency to distort the allocation of resources. If used, interest equalization taxes need to be designed so as to minimize these side effects.

Evidence and Conclusions

Recent experience shows that many developing countries lack suitable instruments to sterilize persistently large capital inflows. When they liberalize markets, these countries often find that raditional sterilization tools are no longer effective, but that they have yet to develop the infrastructure needed for more advanced market-based controls to be applied. Thus, although the long-term objective must be to work towards a fully market-based approach, there remains a short-term case for using a "belts and braces" policy, including supplementary measures and, sometimes, indirect capital controls, as part of a second-best approach.

Statistics indicate that capital mobility is rising in the six countries studied, but is not yet so high as to make efforts at sterilization futile. Given the practical limits to open market operations, including high fiscal costs, all these countries have found it necessary to take supplementary measures. Some measures, such as changes in discount window policy and reserve requirements, have been used more than others, such as foreign exchange swaps and switching government deposits. Sometimes, the use of these little-used methods has been effective, such as with foreign exchange swaps in Indonesia (1990).

In many cases, the scale and persistence of capital inflows has been such that policymakers have also turned to other measures, including wider exchange rate bands, direct intervention in the forward exchange market, and policies to encourage offsetting capital outflows. Some have also adopted indirect capital controls, such as variable deposit requirements and interest equalization taxes.

Empirical tests in industrial countries have often found that using capital controls for sterilization purposes has been largely ineffective. In developing countries, however, the statistical evidence so far (at least from this admittedly small sample) is somewhat more positive. Indirect controls are less distortionary and more transparent than direct restrictions, although they do have disadvantages, including the potential to distort resource allocation, as well as administration costs. Nevertheless, the evidence shows that the use of variable deposit requirements, such as in Spain (1987 and 1989), and interest equalization taxes (although the only recent example is Brazil) can have at least some temporary effect in reducing capital inflows.

The Economic Issues Series

1. *Growth in East Asia: What We Can and What We Cannot Infer.* Michael Sarel. 1996.

2. *Does the Exchange Rate Regime Matter for Inflation and Growth?* Atish R. Ghosh, Anne-Marie Gulde, Jonathan D. Ostry, and Holger Wolf. 1996.

3. *Confronting Budget Deficits.* 1996.

4. *Fiscal Reforms That Work.* C. John McDermott and Robert F. Wescott. 1996.

5. *Transformations to Open Market Operations: Developing Economies and Emerging Markets.* Stephen H. Axilrod. 1996.

6. *Why Worry About Corruption?* Paolo Mauro. 1997.

7. *Sterilizing Capital Inflows.* Jang-Yung Lee. 1997.